Democracy Needs Religion

T0112943

Democracy Needs Religion

Hartmut Rosa

Translated by Valentine A. Pakis
With a Preface by Charles Taylor

polity

Originally published in German as *Demokratie braucht Religion. Über ein eigentümliches Resonanzverhältnis* © 2022 by Kösel Verlag, a division of Penguin Random House Verlagsgruppe GmbH, München, Germany.

This English translation © Polity Press, 2024

Polity Press
65 Bridge Street
Cambridge CB2 1UR, UK

Polity Press
111 River Street
Hoboken, NJ 07030, USA

ISBN-13: 978-1-5095-6122-3 – hardback
ISBN-13: 978-1-5095-6123-0 – paperback

A catalogue record for this book is available from the British Library.
Library of Congress Control Number: 2023939815

Typeset in 12.5 on 15pt Adobe Garamond
by Cheshire Typesetting Ltd, Cuddington, Cheshire
Printed and bound in Great Britain by TJ Books Ltd, Padstow, Cornwall

The publisher has used its best endeavors to ensure that the URLs for external websites referred to in this book are correct and active at the time of going to press. However, the publisher has no responsibility for the websites and can make no guarantee that a site will remain live or that the content is or will remain appropriate.

Every effort has been made to trace all copyright holders, but if any have been overlooked the publisher will be pleased to include any necessary credits in any subsequent reprint or edition.

For further information on Polity, visit our website:
politybooks.com

Contents

Preface

Our contemporary civilization has reached an unprecedented level and intensity of control over our natural environments. We are becoming more and more aware of this and its potential (catastrophic) downsides. But the instrumental stance to the world is hard to shake. It's not just that we are attached to the results. This way of treating nature has produced spectacular growth, and thus more and more of the goods and services we desire. It is also that, once astride the galloping horse of growth, it is increasingly hard to dismount.

In path-breaking work over the last decade, Hartmut Rosa has shown some of the features of our societies and economies that make it very difficult to change course. One of the most important is the one he calls "dynamic stabilization": our contemporary industrial societies can only retain their stability by growing – and, indeed, at a faster and faster pace. This is a tendency built in to our globalized capitalist economy. Globalization permits us to make and sell products more cheaply, and thus to more consumers. We in the rich countries of the West can do this by having them produced in whole and in part in the less affluent countries of Asia. But to pull this off, we have to make huge investments in transport: containers, ships, ports. Otherwise, our economies will grind to a halt – as we saw in the bottlenecks which occurred in the supply chains as we emerged from the pandemic. Growth (in sales) forced growth (in the means of transport).

But this is not the only way that growth generates more growth. Some people's skills become relatively less in demand as the economy develops, and other skills are needed. People have to be retrained (or new entrants have to acquire the new skills). Failure to respond to this requirement means not only bottlenecks, but also unemployment, hence widespread dissatisfaction, which threatens sociopolitical stability.

In all these ways, growth impels more growth. There are systemic mechanisms at work here. And we haven't even begun to consider the subjective side: how mass production can tempt us to possess more (furniture, books, records, iPhones, etc.), and how cheap air travel can induce us to take holidays in exotic places hitherto out of the question for us.

Hartmut has charted some of the downsides to this. Greater opportunities tempt us to do more things, travel to more places, undertake more tasks. We find ourselves chronically short of time, over-committed, and striving to keep the pace, catch up. To-do lists lengthen beyond any possible fulfillment of the tasks they enumerate. Often, that way lies burnout, a very common complaint in our time.

But, beyond specific psychic catastrophes such as burnout, Rosa wants to make us aware that we are closing the door on the deepest, most important human fulfillments. The phrenetic stance of control inhibits our capacity to be interpellated, moved by the world we experience – interpellated as we are by music, for instance, or poetry, or visual art. Or riveted at the sight or scent or feel of nature in a cultivated field or in the wild. Rosa has a word for this kind of experience: "resonance." These experiences resonate in us; there is an affinity here which is *felt*.

We are getting close to understanding the title of this book: *Democracy Needs Religion*. Why these terms? First, why "democracy"? Because we feel as though this mode of government, which is very important to us and cherished by those who live in democracies, is under threat, externally (Putin) and internally (Trump and his counterparts elsewhere). This mode requires, calls for, listening – listening attentively and openly to grasp what our fellow citizens feel, aspire to, are appalled by. For all the messages that are exchanged in our public "debates," we find a decreased willingness to listen, to take in what is really going on in the other. Politics approaches the mindset of civil war. And in our age, which has seen the mass migration of refugees as well as serious attempts to realize the ethic of rights and equality inscribed in our constitutions, the issues turn around who really belongs: who are really American, or quintessential first-class Americans, or Frenchmen, or Britons, Québécois, Hungarian, etc. Tempers and hatreds flare up, and we need ever more "listening hearts," the term Rosa borrows from King Solomon.

Then, why "religion"? Is religion the only zone where resonance can come about? I am sure Rosa doesn't think that. But there is an element of provocation in the use of this term; there are certainly many people today who resonate with, say, nature, who have either consciously turned their back on religion or were never drawn to it. So what is Rosa saying here? Maybe I'm wrong, but I interpret him in the following way: He wants to challenge the notion (shared by both some believers and some non-believers) that a sharp line can be drawn between religion and unbelief. But the feeling of awe that a "secular" person might feel, standing on the edge of a primeval forest, and the awe felt by the believer entering Chartres Cathedral, are not all that far apart. And what those who rarely enter a church may feel when they attend Christmas midnight Mass? This may be hard to situate, because it's on the boundary of the religious and non-religious.

So the message of the book might read: Citizens of today's democracies, listen – the only antidote to your self-enclosing, self-damaging obsessions (with control, with growth, with *more*) is openness to interpellation by resonant experiences.

Charles Taylor

Democracy Needs Religion

Ladies and Gentlemen,*

First, I would like to thank you sincerely for inviting me to the reception today at your diocese. It's a matter close to my heart to enter into dialogue with people of various backgrounds, convictions, and orientations, for my experience has shown that such dialogue can indeed be extremely fruitful. This is especially true for the ways in which I've developed my own theories, which have benefited from being challenged from a wide variety of perspectives and experiences. In fact, I've often

---

* This text is based on an extended and revised version of a lecture delivered to the Diocese of Würzburg, 2022.

noticed that many ideas that required great effort for me to conceive as a sociologist, especially when it comes to resonant relationships, have already been formulated in a theological context. It is often the case, moreover, that such relationships are then put into *practice* in religious settings. I'm therefore all the more pleased to have the opportunity to discuss things with you here today and engage in conversation.

Many heartfelt thanks, too, not only for the kind introductory words but also for the gloriously beautiful music at the beginning of this event. When thinking about resonance, one could hardly find better inspiration than a flute or woodwind ensemble, and this is simply because resonances become directly audible and physically palpable in their presence. Music produced in this way literally causes the material, social, and spiritual conditions around us to vibrate. In a sense, our breath begins to resonate with the instruments, but also with the musicians themselves, with the room, and with each other as listening and meaning-processing beings.

Much in the same vein – and I would like to congratulate you directly for this – is the motto chosen by the diocese this year: *Give me a listening heart.* This is a passage from the Bible, from I Kings 3:9. Yet it also applies, I think, to the central idea of my book on resonance, which is this: *A listening, receptive, and responsive heart* is precisely what we need as a society and as individuals to lead successful individual lives and to enjoy a successful coexistence. However, the fact that this appeal has to be made implies that the heart may not be willing to listen, that it is hardly a matter of course that we will allow ourselves to be addressed. And if the heart fails to listen, this might not be the fault of an individual alone – it can also be attributed to certain social conditions that are themselves unhearing and make us so. In order for music to resonate with us, for instance, the spatial, temporal, and social conditions have to be just right – and we ourselves have to be in the right disposition. In terms of the music here today, this means first of all that the flutes and other wind instruments have to be in a state of resonance with each other. If they are out of tune, things have already become difficult. Not impossible, however, because the uncontrollability of resonance means not only that it might fail to occur even in optimal conditions, but also that it is possible in unlikely circumstances. Then, however, things become even more difficult. Even the contextual conditions have to be right: When we happen to be in a bad mood or when, while listening, we happen to be in an aggressive or combative state of mind, then even the most beautiful music will fail to reach us. It might even make us feel more withdrawn.

For resonance to occur, in other words, it's safe to say that many preconditions need to be met, and this is true not only here in regard to music, but also in society at large. And this is especially the case in today's late-modern society, whose condition, as I've argued elsewhere, might best be described as a *frenetic standstill*. This expression is meant to imply two things. On the one hand, society is accelerating. Indeed, it is frantically rushing ahead; for structural reasons, in fact, it must rush in this way to maintain its structure. On the other hand, however, it has become mired or sclerotic. It has lost the sense of its historical (forward) momentum. This conflicted situation is, in a way, a core insight that informs much of my research as a sociologist.

When a society functions in the mode of dynamic stabilization, which is my term for this condition, it is permanently forced to grow,

accelerate, push things forward, produce innovation after innovation, and more or less strive
for disruptive change. If in doing so, however,
it loses the sense of forward momentum that
we've understood for centuries as progress, then
it will find itself in a crisis situation. And the
exciting question now is this: Does such a society need a religious foundation or orientation;
does it even need religious institutions such as
churches? I would like to think about this with
you today, because this question is relevant not
only in ecclesiastical contexts but from a sociolog-
ical perspective as well: Does a modern, secular,
capitalist society in any way need religious ideas,
practices, and conceptions, because such things
might (alone) be able to touch the heart in such
a way that it becomes willing to listen? Or is that
just an anachronism? Aren't religions precisely
that which closes our hearts to others? Aren't
churches, in the end, no more than a vestige from
a different and bygone form of society, remnants
from a different way of relating to the world?

Following this line of argumentation, one can
quickly find good reasons to say: Yes, religion, at
least in its institutionalized form, really no longer
suits our age of DIY religiosity, where everyone

somehow constructs a worldview of his own; where what we have, if nothing else, is religious pluralism, in which very many different voices offer very different interpretations. My students often say this. Sure, they say, there are all sorts of different superstitions out there, and religion is one of them. This is certainly one way to interpret the present. At the very least, we can say that there's a multitude of religious offerings and interpretations of the world and that the state should not attribute any particular importance to organized religious institutions, because to do so is to violate the principle of neutrality. Why, for instance, do we have a work-free Sunday in central Europe (not to mention North and South America), when Sunday is a holy day only for Christians, whereas Friday is holy for Muslims, Saturday for those of the Jewish faith, and whatever other days are sacred to other believers? Wouldn't it be better for everyone to take a day off whenever he or she wanted? When it comes to difficulties, this is just the beginning. The same question can of course be asked about holidays such as Christmas, and regarding schools in Germany: Why are Catholic and Protestant theology offered as course subjects, but not hippiedom or *hygge*? These questions come to mind in general, and they are also posed and genuinely discussed in political contexts. One can even argue that church is perhaps a disruptive factor in society, for the insistence on having Sundays off creates a disadvantage to Germany's global economic competitiveness. And if religious institutions also constantly raise objections against progress – by arguing that stem cells, for instance, should not be used in research because they are somehow sacred or God-given – then this is likewise a disadvantage in the global competition. The view of many people, and of many social scientists in particular, is that religion makes us conservative and burdens us with economic disadvantages. To them, church is an anachronism that has no place in today's ideological reservoir and clashes with the self-perception of a modern society. Moreover, they might add that it's an anachronism that is a blatantly moral and ethical problem, as is clear from ongoing abuses of power and the thousands of sexual abuses that have been committed and covered up by religious authorities. This is one way to approach the question posed at the beginning of my lecture. The answer to the question of whether modern society needs religious ideas, practices, or institutions would then be a curt and simple: No! By their very nature, religious institutions are undemocratic, backward-thinking, authoritarian, and permeated by power structures that open doors to abuse, on the one hand, and, on the other hand, constantly cause people of different faiths to fight against each other and close themselves off to one another, instead of encountering one another with listening hearts. And, to be honest, I'm sometimes left with the rather concerning impression that certain church officials even share this opinion, that they regard *themselves* as superfluous, retrograde, and indeed problematic.

Sometimes I'm a little shocked when I talk to people who attend church or are religiously engaged, and perhaps even hold positions of responsibility within these institutions. I'm a little shocked because I've heard more than one of them say something like this: "Yes, that's just the way it is now. No one really wants to hear from us anymore, and we also have the feeling that perhaps we have nothing to say in response to the present crises." And, in fact, we do have to wonder: What did religious institutions have to say or offer during the debates about the coronavirus? Regarding the question of vaccine mandates, where did they stand – yes or no? Should schools be closed? Yes or no? Or today: weapons to Ukraine, peace negotiations – yes or no? Do churches or other religious institutions have a strong voice or function? Do they still have any religious authority that might allow them to say something relevant to society that might otherwise be left unsaid? If we are offered no significant guidance of any sort and are met instead with silence, then we have to conclude that church and religion no longer have anything to say.

An interesting crisis indicator was recently brought to my attention by someone in the ecclesiastical sphere, and this took place at a celebration held by a theological faculty. When asked about his profession, this person told me that it's been more than 30 years since he was proud to say that he worked in the context of the church. Today, he said, this is something he's rather ashamed to admit or tries to avoid mentioning, claiming instead that he works for a charitable organization. This is extremely revealing to me, because if church dignitaries attempt to conceal what they do (professionally, at least), then one thing is very clear: The churches have a problem, and a big one at that. And we all know that these churches have contributed immensely to their own loss of reputation by abusing, for centuries, this very reputation and their very authority for the most shameful of things – for sexual and economic and political exploitation. It's by no means my intention to gloss over any of this. I'm a sociologist, after all, and I'm not blind!

Nevertheless, what I would like to do today – and I would like to do so not as a religious person but as a sociologist – is to persuade you that religion and perhaps even church have a *damn* important role to play in our modern society (and I hope you can forgive my language in the present context). The simple reason why I believe this is my conviction that they have something to offer that our society urgently needs; I believe, in other words, that they have access to certain resources that might help us find our way out of the frenetic standstill in which we presently exist. I believe that they make certain ways of relating to the world conceivable, imaginable, and tangible, and that these ways differ from the aggressive mode of living that prevails under the conditions of modern capitalism. A society that finds itself in a breathless, frenetic stand-still pays a rather high social, psychological, and economic price to maintain its structural conditions. It's long been observed that this society is desperately searching for an alternative form of relating to the world, of *being-in-the-world*. Where can this society look for different ways to relate to life, to the universe itself, to the cosmos, to nature? Where can we find this alternative reservoir, and how might religion play a role in this pursuit?

In what follows, I would like to make the case that we as a society are in a serious crisis and that we absolutely need religious institutions, traditions, practices, belief structures, convictions, and rites in order to extricate ourselves from it. My basic thought, which I want to make clear right away, is that our society is severely lacking in listening hearts – politically and in all other possible respects as well. For this reason, we need ideas, practices, and whatever else we can find that might reveal to us and allow us to experience what this could really mean – what it might really mean to have a listening heart. My argument is that a partial answer to this question, at least, can be found in religious contexts.

Before delving into this, I have to begin by offering a more precise diagnosis of contemporary society. It's true, of course, that I've often spoken about this, but I would like to rehearse my assessment yet again, and perhaps even express it in more pointed terms.

Many of my colleagues maintain that there is no such thing as society in the singular; instead, there are *political* events and processes and institutions – just as there are economic, religious, legal, and athletic events and processes and institutions – and all of these coexist alongside one another. I believe, however, that the term *society* can be used as a collective singular, that there really is something like a totality of society in which different institutions and people work together and mutually influence one another. My term for the fundamental form of this society – for its cultural and structural formation – is dynamic stabilization. This is how I define a modern society. A society is modern when it can only stabilize itself in a dynamic way or, in other words, when it systematically and structurally depends on permanent growth in order to reproduce itself and preserve the institutional status quo.

It is not my position that it is somehow historically special that our society is accelerating. Regarding this point, I have often butted heads with historians who are quick to point out to me that there have been earlier societies characterized by acceleration, that there have been other eras of rapid acceleration, and that periods of growth can also be found in non-modern contexts. And yes, of course, if we look at population growth or the development of civilization, we really do see something like an acceleration curve, so that it's possible to say that modern society is just part of a long-term historical trend of growth and acceleration.

What's special about modern society, according to my definition, is thus not *the fact that* society is growing – its population, say, or its economic production – or that it is accelerating in many respects. Rather, what's special about it is that it *must* keep growing and accelerating in order to maintain its status quo. In fact, this can be quite easily understood with reference to Max Weber, who pointed out that most premodern societies we know of were subsistence societies. They had a very precise sense of what was needed to survive. We need this amount of bread or that amount of grain to make it through the winter; a certain amount of heating material, a solid house, some clothing, perhaps two pairs of pants, and maybe candles or torches and oil for religious worship – and then we have what we need. And these are things that we restore when they run short or fall apart: When our pants have holes or rips, we darn them, and when we can no longer repair them in this way, we replace them with an identical pair of pants. Of course, what we need includes not only our house and nutrition and clothing but also – depending on the historical and cultural context – items for religious worship, for rites, for the temple, or for priests. But there is always a sure sense of what one needs, even if this sense gradually changes over the course of history. Why does it change? In part because of environmental conditions: sometimes an enemy is at the gate, sometimes the climate changes, sometimes there's a shortage of a certain raw material that we need. All of this then drives innovation, and of course there is also the fact that people are curious. They want to try out new things, and sometimes they discover something exciting, something that makes their life easier, and if this discovery turns out to be really good, it will often be adopted as a cultural innovation and find its way into other communities.

Anyone who thinks historically about societies will see that they've never been static. They are always affected by innovation and change, and often the latter have something to do with acceleration and growth. I think that Ian Morris and others are right when they say that it's helpful to examine the energy budget of societies (that is, input versus output). People need energy to generate energy. Food is the most important form of energy, and then of course there's also heat – at least in northern or temperate areas – and thus the decisive question has long been: How and where can we get enough energy to survive through the winter? Or simply to survive at all? For thousands of years, as historians have noted, human beings have had to use all the energy at their disposal in order to achieve the goal of survival, or at least to survive adequately, according to their respective cultural notion of adequacy. And therefore it makes sense that when a discovery is made, perhaps out of mere curiosity, this discovery will be extremely consequential if it enables people to achieve the same energy output with less energy input. So, for example, when we began to cook, fry, or bake food – or even a step before, when controllable fire was discovered – we were able to harness the same amount of energy for our metabolism with much less expenditure. And when people notice something as advantageous as this, they obviously keep doing it. In this way, with the help of history, it's possible to reconstruct fairly accurately how it became possible to release more and more energy with the same or even less energy input from human bodies. Morris's term for this is *energy capture*. Of course, the goal of acquiring exactly the energy I need with *less* physical effort is one of the main principles of innovation.

I have therefore never argued that earlier societies were static. Historically, however, our present society has the completely novel problem that it needs to expend *more and more* energy in order to maintain its existing conditions. I would say – and Max Weber saw things the same way – that this truly is structurally and systematically irrational. The clearest example is the economy. Whether you're a business or a state, a city or a country, the EU or whatever else – you need to be in a state of *permanent growth* in order to maintain your position. In other words, you have to achieve economic growth, increase productivity, and constantly strive to innovate, optimize, and streamline. We are witnesses to this right now. In the new German "traffic light" government, all three parties are in agreement: "We need growth!" "The engine of growth must be set in motion!" "We intend to grow out of this crisis!" These are the words of the German chancellor, Olaf Scholz. As an economic liberal, the Finance Minister Christian Lindner is a big fan of growth by default, and even the Greens are now on board. And I'm asking you and the politicians rather directly: *In which area, exactly, do you want growth?* I would really like to discuss this with these gentlemen. Where do you want to grow? Should we buy more cars? I don't want to question the fact that Mercedes, BMW, and Volkswagen benefit from producing and selling more cars every year. Of course, they say it's a good year when they sell more vehicles. Or larger vehicles with more horsepower and more tonnage or something; more value needs to be produced, but this can only really be achieved by selling *more* cars and *more* trucks. For every one of these companies, stagnation is an alarm signal. We can have all the Green fantasies that we want, but the fact of the matter is that the automobile industry remains one of the central growth industries in Germany.

Robert Habeck, the Green Minister for Economic Affairs, might perhaps say to this: "No, I don't want to see any growth in the automobile industry," but my question back to him would be: perhaps in the airline industry?! Because we're growing there too, and perhaps even fastest of all; the number of aircraft and the number of flights and the passenger numbers have all been going almost straight up – at least before the coronavirus. But today? And against the backdrop of the climate crisis? In this case, striving for systematic growth seems like an extraordinarily stupid idea.

OK, so cars and airplanes are off the table. Should we perhaps build more houses? At the moment, the construction industry is booming, so much so that there's talk of a construction bubble, but then if you look at the effects of surface sealing (covering the ground with impervious surfaces, in other words), you'll see that this is an enormous problem. More and more surfaces are being settled and sealed. In tiny Switzerland alone, a surface the size of nearly seven football fields is sealed off every day (!). Over the course of a year, this will amount to a surface area as large as 2,500 football fields. Moreover, ecologically catastrophic energy consumption is being driven up every day by the ever increasing living space that people seem to need and by the increasing number of houses being built. In the long run, to say that we want to see growth in the construction industry is also not a good idea, though this industry is of the utmost importance to the economy.

So I suppose we ought to grow in other sectors, even though there aren't many left. Computers and smartphones, perhaps? The very goods that are being replaced faster and faster? Every two years, we throw away billions of these devices. This is hardly a good thing in light of rare earth metals, coltan, lithium, and other dwindling resources. But it's not just a bad thing because the mining industry has to dig deeper and deeper into the earth to extract raw materials; it's also bad because we're producing more and more toxic garbage to fill up our already overflowing landfills. In the end, anyone with half a brain would say: "Nope, we're not really looking to grow in this sector either."

The next suggestion would be that we should grow in the food industry. There are still many people in the world who are hungry, and most of the food that we throw away isn't especially harmful to the environment, though it's possible to argue otherwise with respect to the meat industry. Here, however, the problem lies elsewhere. Those of us who can actually buy the food (and therefore spur the necessary growth) are already overweight. This is the case in all Western countries! All the societies that can produce more food suffer from obesity. This is a plain and simple fact, and do you know what the food industry is doing about it? Its plan is to keep growing by inserting enzymes or additives that shut down the satiety signal between the stomach and the brain so that we continue eating even when we're already full. What further evidence is needed to demonstrate that, in the Anthropocene, the mode of dynamic stabilization has become downright suicidal?!

In short, the problem is that we have to keep growing in all these sectors or else jobs will be lost, even though the fact of the matter is that the ongoing pursuit of this growth agenda stopped making sense a long time ago. It doesn't matter which branch of the economy is under discussion. Look at the clothing industry. We throw everything away even if it's still good and wearable – countless items of clothing and pairs of shoes are thrown into the trash even if they've hardly been worn (if worn at all). For this alone, every culture before ours would call us insane. We throw things away simply because they're no longer fashionable. The pharmaceutical industry is constantly growing as well, and this is a good thing with respect to the quick development of vaccines, as we recently witnessed during the pandemic. In fact, proponents of growth almost invariably refer to the pharmaceutical industry to show that growth and innovation are beneficial to humankind, but even this can be called into question if one considers for a moment the growing field of cosmetic surgery or other surgical procedures that make no medical sense but are economically profitable. I don't want to say that society should *never* grow or accelerate or innovate. What I want to say is that it shouldn't always *have to grow* in order to maintain the status quo. I find it truly absurd at this point to speak abstractly of growth without indicating where this growth should be achieved. When we ask concrete questions about where, exactly, we should grow, we never receive a good answer. At best, we'll hear something about *green technologies*, but this is just a way to sidestep the rather substantial issue at hand, given that advances in this small sector will never lead to the growth rates that are needed and expected.

Even more absurd is the fact that we, as humans, don't even want all this growth because we're greedy and insatiable. We need it because, without growth, we could no longer sustain the entire existing social structure. Growth and acceleration are driven by fear, not by greed. They are not driven by our growing needs but rather by our concern that if we fail to grow, we won't be able to meet our *existing* needs. If we decide today to stop growing, companies will go out of business overnight and there will be masses of unemployed people. Then, in turn, the government's tax revenues will shrink while its spending levels will simultaneously increase because, for example, we will have to build better infrastructure to reignite growth. Above all, however, government spending will have to increase because all the people out of work will have to be paid. We would not be able to pay our rent or maintain the healthcare system; the entire care sector would become even more dramatically underfinanced, and cultural and educational institutions would lose financial backing as well. Greece's disastrous financial and economic crisis after 2007, the effects of which can still be felt today, provided a clear illustration of this chain reaction.

Thus the entire system depends on growth, year after year. And wherever such growth is impossible, we have to speed things up all the more and optimize production processes even more relentlessly. Take the example of Japan. The country experienced many years of little if any growth, but this only increased the pressure there to accelerate and become more efficient. This is logical enough, because if all companies are producing and selling more cars, then it doesn't matter much whether one is the market leader or in second place. The pie, that is, is getting bigger for everyone. If the overall pie is no longer growing, however, then you have to be the cheapest on the market – and the fastest. This is why the pressure to escalate is even greater when growth is lacking, at least as long as the economy is operating in the mode of dynamic stabilization.

The consequence is as follows: We live in a system in which we – as individuals, as institutions, and as society at large – *must* become faster in order to maintain our position in the social order. We *must* accelerate, we *must* be innovative – be the first to have the new product, the first to have more efficient modes of production. We have to grow to preserve the status quo. In essence, this is simply the logic of generalized competition. This also means, however, that we have to expend more physical energy every year, whether from wind, the sun, coal, nuclear power, or wherever else. We need to use more and more energy to keep the growth game going or, in other words, to keep things the way they are.

By this point, I hope, the irrationality of our society is as clear as day. I don't think there's ever been a way of life that organized itself in such a way that it needs *more* energy every year to pre-serve the status quo. Keep in mind Ian Morris and his idea of energy capture. As I said earlier: Historically, change has always taken place when it became possible to achieve more with the same amount of energy or to achieve the same yield with less energy. But a society that is system-atically and structurally set up in such a way that it needs to invest, use, and "capture" *more and more* energy in order to maintain what already exists? This is perverse. And it's not only physical energy that needs to be expended, but also political energy. Politicians and political programs are constantly motivating, challenging, and encouraging us. The elderly should remobilize and contribute to the workforce; the youth should no longer take 12 or 10 semesters to complete a university degree, but only 6, etc. You see this on every level, and I don't even blame the politicians for this. If I were a politician, I'd presumably do the same thing.

One might think that this constant investment and escalation of political and physical energy would be enough to achieve our aims, but it's not. As human beings, we are also systematically forced to invest more and more of our mental energy in the growth game. After all, acceleration, growth, and innovation are not accomplished by systems or machines; these things are accomplished by us! Yes, *we the people* have to move faster next year than we did this year. In this respect, I would argue that our social establishment or orientation has created an *aggressive relationship* to the world. I believe, in fact, that we can all feel this in our own bodies, and the pandemic in particular made this feeling all the more palpable.

Our relationship to the world is aggressive; we are always in attack mode or alarm mode. Why? The most obvious answer is that our to-do lists have exploded in size. Every year, we have to do a little more and take on more tasks. On scales large and small, our relationship to the world has become aggressive. On the large scale – on the macro-level of life – we are, of course, faced above all with the ecological crisis. Industries are behaving more and more recklessly, drilling deeper and deeper for oil, mining for rare earth metals, copper, lithium, coltan, and for whatever else can be extracted from the ground. In so doing, they pollute our sphere of life. This has systematically created an aggressive relationship to the environment. On the meso-level of our existence, the social level, we can see this growing aggression in politics, for instance. If you live precariously and in a frenzy – and the politics of neoliberalism has ensured that just about every form of existence feels precarious – and all you hear all day long is "We have to grow, we have to do better," then someone with a different opinion, who constantly wants something different and is hard to understand and loves different things and believes different things – this person is no more than an obstacle. In fact, he should keep his big mouth shut.

My colleague Michael Bruter at the London School of Economics recently published an interesting study. In it he shows that the unsettling thing about democracies is that the political culture has seemed to change in a troubling way. Those with different political opinions are no longer simply viewed as dialogue partners with whom one might engage in debate; instead, they're regarded as loathsome enemies who need to be silenced. The paradigmatic example of this is the United States, where it's clear to see in the ways that Republicans and Democrats perceive one another and behave toward one another. "Lock her up," for example, was what Republicans shouted about Hillary Clinton. This was likewise clear to see in England, especially in the relationship between Brexiteers and Remainers. One side was doggedly *in favor* of leaving the EU, while the other side was absolutely *against* it. In the German-speaking countries, we witnessed something similar in the conflict between anti-vaxxers and vaccine supporters. No matter where we look, we no longer have any fruitful debates about how we want to live or how we ought to structure our respective ways of life; the prevailing mood is that it's not worth listening to others, because they're simply irrational haters or dangerous traitors. The other side should shut up, in other words; we treat them more and more as enemies who need to be silenced, and this is the case on both sides of the political spectrum. Left-wingers regard right-wingers as fascists, racists, anti-Semites, and misanthropes, while right-wingers regard lefties as traitors and unthinking zombies. So this is what we see: Our aggressive relationship to the world, which derives from our never-ending and insatiable compulsion to accelerate and grow, has spilled over into politics. In the meantime, this social aggression has once again even made war a real course of action in Europe. As the dominant mode of relating to the world, however, aggression has effects beyond the macro-level of ecology and the meso-level of society – it has also seeped into the micro-level of our individual lives and psyches.

This is reflected, I think, in what we call burnout or the burnout crisis. This phenomenon has been growing rather dramatically and, according to the latest data, it's been made even worse by the coronavirus pandemic. In almost every society, the media have been issuing constant reports about this, and all the new numbers and statistics seem to demonstrate that there's a "mental-health crisis" going on, especially among teens and university students, but not within these groups alone. I cite the media here not as evidence of the clinical extent of this mental illness, but as an important indicator of society's fear of it. Often, when speaking to a large audience, I'll ask a question that might be of some interest here as well: How many of you sometimes say to yourselves, or have at least recently thought something like, "I really have to slow down a little next year" or "I have to reduce some of my responsibilities, or else I'll suffer from burnout" or "I'm in danger of burning out"? When I ask this question, it almost always happens that nearly everyone in the room raises a hand. This has been the case regardless of whether I'm speaking to students, professionals, or even to retirees. The sense that "things can't carry on in this way" has become a culturally dominant feeling. I can say this quite confidently even if the rising number of medical leaves taken due to burnout have yet to be confirmed in objective scientific analyses. We know, of course, that we have to pay attention to such statistics. Nevertheless, I think that the feverish discourse itself has already made it pretty clear that there's a crisis going on. And, interestingly enough, what we're dealing with on the macro-level and the micro-level is, strictly speaking, an energy problem: We're overheating the atmosphere and creating heat in the climate through our increasing use of physical energy, and we're overheating in our own lives through our excessive use of mental energy. The system of dynamic stabilization has created an energy problem in the climate and an energy problem in our psyches: Both are burning out.

Before moving on, I would like to make a final important point about how my notion of the *frenetic standstill* should be understood. I am convinced, as I mentioned at the beginning, that this situation has become as urgent as it is because we have lost our historical and cultural sense of forward momentum or progress. I don't want in any way to deny that modernity's growth agenda has been both efficient and highly attractive for a long time. In fact, we can't express enough gratitude for this agenda, which has given rise to unbelievable economic welfare, scientific knowledge, and technological capabilities. The logic of dynamic stabilization has led to progress on many levels of human existence. To the critics of this system on the left, I would say that your critiques are toothless if you ignore these gains, because it seems fairly obvious to me that the market and capitalism have been essential to the creation of all the opportunities and resources that we have at our disposal today. That said, it needs to be acknowledged that this system has, from the beginning, been associated with a number of quasi-religious ideas and promises. On account of increased productivity – as Marx rightly observed and Marcuse argued further (all of Critical Theory, in fact, emphasizes this point repeatedly) – it has essentially become possible to measure existence according to its utility value. The promise was that we would become so successful at processing nature and overcoming scarcity that we would no longer struggle for survival in our daily lives, that we would no longer need to harbor any fears about losing our place or so-called legitimacy in the world or becoming superfluous. The promise, in short, was that we would no longer need to worry about our existence because scarcity would become a thing of the past. This was, of course, a great promise! And an equally great promise was that scientific progress would make ignorance disappear: "We'll figure out how to live properly!" And by "live properly," I mean something like "give birth properly" and "love properly" or "sleep properly" and "eat properly." And even beyond all this, the growth agenda offered yet another promise: "Through our achievements in greater efficiency, we will overcome the scarcity of time; we will have an excess of (life)time!"

Meanwhile, however, it's become obvious that not a single one of these promises has even remotely been fulfilled. In fact, the opposite seems to have happened. To be honest, no one believes any more – not even the proponents of growth in our "traffic-light" government – that things have improved in any relevant respect. Global competition will become much fiercer as the climate crisis progresses, and this problem will be made all the worse by other countries catching up to us. *We will all have to be prepared for things becoming much tougher in light of growing competition and dwindling resources.* This has long been the message heard from economic circles – and now plague and war have reentered the modern conversation. Plague and war – these are the proto-scourges of humanity. Didn't we think that such things had been overcome, or were at least on the verge of being overcome? Epidemics and wars, even if they still existed here and there, were an emblem of the past. Now in the year 2023, however, they suddenly seem emblematic of the present and the future. It is no less interesting that all the developments discussed above have created more instead of less uncertainty, especially at the intersection between scientific knowledge and the ways we lead our lives. Never before has there been more uncertainty, for instance, about what, when, and how people should eat or shouldn't eat. Think about the insanity surrounding the question of who can or cannot tolerate certain types of food. It's truly absurd. Today we know more than ever about the relationship between nutrition and our bodies, and yet we have no idea anymore about what we should or shouldn't eat. I always thought, for example, that eating a lot of fat was bad because it would cause me to gain weight, but recently I read that it's actually good to eat a lot of fat – even for those desiring to lose weight. I also recently read that consuming too much sugar doesn't cause diabetes at all! Take any example you want – in the end, people don't even really know what they should eat or not. Anyone who has to deal with children is familiar with this. One of them will say "Well, I can't eat that"; another will say "I'm not allowed to eat that"; others will say "I'm not allowed to eat that with that," "I'm expected to eat in the morning," "I avoid breakfast," "I try to go twelve hours without eating." In short, we don't know anymore! An activity as simple and natural as eating has plunged us into a state of uncertainty and confusion.

This can also be illustrated with another example – an example which I, as a man, should approach with the utmost humility. Nevertheless, I find it interesting, and the topic I have in mind is pregnancy. We see that the fear of giving birth seems only to *increase* as we learn more about it. This is related to a feeling of growing powerlessness, because now it's the *medical devices* – the ultrasound, for instance – that tells a woman in labor what to do and how the child is faring. Her own sense of things no longer matters anymore. Regarding childbirth, in other words, we apparently know less today than we knew centuries – or even millennia – ago.

This form of non-knowledge is increasing everywhere, with the incidental consequence that people have begun to feel increasingly unsatisfied with themselves. An interesting study has shown that, before the fall of the Berlin Wall, people in East Germany felt – and some continue to feel so today – much more comfortable in their own skin than people in West Germany. The feeling of not being good enough, of not being content with one's body and mind, of having to change oneself completely – this feeling is constantly increasing. We have long given up the hope that permanent growth and optimization will allow us to lead the good life and enjoy a successful relationship to the world. We have finally recognized that this promise will not be fulfilled. Nevertheless, the German "traffic-light" government, the EU, and the United States all want growth to continue unabated. And the opposition has nothing else to offer.

Modernity – the modern social system – was so successful and so promising because, and as long as, people had the feeling that they were working toward a better future. You can see this in data from all Western or early industrialized societies: There and then, parents always lived with the conviction – not only in the upper class but also deep into the middle and working classes – that their hard work, effort, and sacrifices would allow their children to have lives better than their own. This was a strong conviction and motivational force that also created intergenerational resonance or feelings of connection. *We work hard and make many sacrifices, but our children will be much better off.* This conviction is dead, and it's dead not only in the West but also in developed Asian countries. Everywhere we look – and Silicon Valley is the bellwether here – both parents and children are saying, "We have to do everything we can to ensure that the next generation won't be much worse off than ours." Rates of suicide and depression are especially high in Silicon Valley right now, because the children there are convinced that they'll never be able to maintain the standard of living that they're used to. Meanwhile, empirical social research from Japan, from the United States, from all over Europe, and from Australia has demonstrated that parents, and even the majority of adults, are convinced that things will be worse for younger generations. To me, this is a decisive point: Culturally and collectively, we are no longer living with the perception and conviction that we're heading toward a promising future; instead, we're running away from an abyss that seems to be catching up to us. This abyss is defined above all by the climate crisis, which is becoming more and more dramatic, but also by the extinction of species, by increased economic competition, and by the return of pestilence and war. This is what I mean by the term *frenetic standstill:* Every year, we have to run faster and faster to avoid falling into the abyss that's chasing us down. But our cultural-historical situation is even worse. Not only have we lost the future – we've also lost the past. Just as it's no longer possible for us to paint a promising picture of the future (when asked about the future, children and adolescents already expect either a world made uninhabitable by ecological disaster or one in which people have been enslaved by AI-driven machines and robots), our view of the past has become rather dim as well. If we think about the history of colonial violence, which is part of modernity as well – if we think about the subjection, subjugation, enslavement, and exploitation of the majority of people by a white minority who preached about human rights and enlightenment but practiced the opposite; if we think about the discrimination against and oppression of women and sexual minorities; and if we think

about the economic exploitation of the working class – then, even in retrospect, the regime
of dynamic stabilization doesn't appear to have
been a story of progress. That church and religion
played an essential part in this history of violence
is by no means in doubt, but I'll return to this
matter shortly. At this point, however, I would
like to stress again that our late-modern present
is in the process of losing both the past and the
future; between the two, we're incapable of creating a resonant relationship that might allow
us to narrate our history as a history of progress
and thereby forge a connection between past and
future generations. This is an essential reason for
our ecological failure: Whenever there's a thread
of resonance linking the past to the future, the
fate of future generations is a "natural" concern
to us, so to speak; this concern arises organically
from our historical sense of being connected.
Whenever this thread of resonance is broken,
however, past generations become just as much
a burden to us (if we're expected to care for their
graves) as future generations (which we regard as
competitors for scarce resources).

In the end, the picture of the present that I'm
trying to depict is rather bleak. Let's therefore

turn our attention at last to how I would like to oppose the regime of dynamic stabilization and the aggressive conditions that have resulted from it; let me also try to explain why I think that we might need religions, and maybe even churches, today perhaps more urgently than ever before. It's safe to say, I think, that *democracy* does not function in a mode of aggression. We can see this in democratic crises around the world today. As I see it, the phrase "Give me a listening heart" therefore has an eminently important political dimension. In fact, it has this same political dimension in the Bible itself. The young Solomon is unexpectedly made a political ruler – a king – by God. In response to this, Solomon prays not for weapons, power, or allies – curiously enough, he prays for a listening heart. Already in the Bible, if you will, the listening heart is a precondition for successful political rule, for good government.

In my earlier work, I repeatedly stressed that democracy is based on a promise and it can only function when everyone has a *voice* that can be heard. More recently, however, I've come to the conviction that our *ears* are just as essential. It's not enough for me to have a voice that's heard; I also need ears to hear the voices of others. And so I would like to agree again with Solomon and say that, in addition to our ears, we also need this listening heart, a heart that *wants* to listen to others and respond to them. Another person should *not* simply shut up because he seems like a traitor or an idiot or an obstacle. I want to listen to this person precisely because he's different. In today's society, in which time is always short and competition is everywhere, it's admittedly rather difficult to adopt this attitude and have a listening heart. More and more, people tend to regard one another as idiots – because they're for or against vaccines, because they want to supply weapons to Ukraine or not, because they're in favor of more gender-inclusive language or not, because they do too much or too little about the climate crisis, etc. Such antagonism weighs especially heavily on democracy, which we've chosen as our political system because the alternatives seem even worse. Democracy is our society's central article of faith, but it needs voices, ears, *and* listening hearts to avoid being dysfunctional. Let's take another look at the dispute about admitting or not admitting migrants. One side says that we've allowed too many refugees to enter the country and that it's treasonous to open the borders to an invasion of violence and criminality. And the other side claims that we ourselves are the criminals for allowing so many refugees to drown and freeze to death at our borders and for being so utterly egotistical and heartless. Both sides had and still have the feeling that the issue is really about fighting against criminals. In disputes of this sort, Max Weber's call for intellectual honesty seems of utmost importance. Intellectual honesty, according to Weber, entails listening and recognizing that there might perhaps be arguments on the other side that have some merit, that speak to me, and that should be taken into consideration. This is the republican understanding of democracy, an understanding that citizens should get together as people who have something to say to one another, and this means not only "I've got something to say *to you*" or "I gave him a piece of *my mind*" but also "*You* also have something to say *to me*" or "I would like to hear from *you*." The republican idea of democracy is that this sort of reciprocal outreach can lead to reciprocal transformations. Interactions of this sort enable us to develop a sense of what Hannah Arendt called *natality*, which is to say that we are all here in this world for the simple reason that we were born.

In other words, we can change, start over, create something new, break out of our old patterns of thought and behavior, and even alter our institutional routines.

Therefore, I would like to say: Democracy needs a *listening heart* in order to function. It needs to be perceptive to (very) different ideas, and it needs to be transformed. Such a listening heart will not, however, fall from the heavens. The attitude associated with it is extremely difficult to adopt in a society as aggressive as our own; under the conditions and pressure of constant growth and optimization, it can even be called an irrational attitude. The thesis that I would like to share with you this evening, therefore, is that religious traditions and institutions such as churches have at their disposal the narratives, cognitive reservoirs, rites, practices, and spaces in which a listening heart might be cultivated and experienced. This is the basic argument that I would like to present to you: *We must allow ourselves to be invoked – spoken to –* if democracy is to succeed. I've been saying this for many years as a sociologist, and when I repeat it now, it's not only because of the motto that your diocese has chosen for this year. At the heart of modernity's crisis lies a *crisis of invocability* and this is just as evident in the crisis of faith as it is in the crisis of democracy. In the words of my colleague Bruno Latour, who sadly passed away recently, I would express this as follows: The most important thing I can do is to stop and listen. This is why one of my favorite German words is *aufhören*. It perfectly suits the concept of the listening heart. On the one hand, this great German word means *to stop*. On the other hand, however, the word means *to listen up* (*auf-hören*). It implies that while I'm working through my to-do list, exhausting myself on the hamster wheel in life's frenetic standstill, I should listen up, be attentive to what's out there, allow myself to be invoked and touched by something different, by a different voice that says something that diverges from my agenda and is not what I expected and thus represents an opportunity to engage with someone in a functional exchange of ideas.

Society – indeed, democracy itself – needs the ability to be addressed and invoked, which is to say that it needs to be able to stop and listen. I have tried to capture the essence of this ability with my concept of resonance, which also implies a different way of relating to the world. If my diagnosis is correct, our fundamental problem is as follows: We are always operating in an aggressive mode, because we always have to work on something or buy something or we want to have something or experience something, and so on. We're either gaining control over things or losing control of things. And we have to ask: Is there not another way to live? Is a different way of relating to the world possible to conceive, experience, and live? Think about listening to music. This activity really has nothing to do with growth, acceleration, or control. Merely *listening* to music? No. Creating music, perhaps – we can argue about that – but when I'm listening to music, I'm simply listening to it. Of course, somehow, I'm still distracted when doing so and feel the need to write a text message or check in on the latest articles in the *Guardian* or the *New York Times*, and these activities really do cause me to stop listening closely to music. But suddenly, out of the blue, I'll pause and listen up! I'll stop and listen because something in the song has reached me or touched me! Music often has this transformative power. Sometimes, when music takes hold of you or when something calls out to you and induces a reaction, it feels like a bodily sensation, as though something has changed your entire physical condition. You really notice it, because it's like a breath of fresh air that brings to life a vivacious relationship to the world. You feel alive, in other words, and it's precisely moments like these that touch me and call out to me. In these moments, I don't know how things will turn out or what it means to be invoked or touched in such ways, but I do know that a resonant moment has begun.

For me, resonance has four defining elements or moments. The first is affection, the feeling of being affected by something – or perhaps one could even call it invocation. Something calls me or addresses me and causes me to stop (and listen), and whatever this something is, it surely can't be something that I've already thought. A transgressive moment comes into play. Resonance is not about pure harmony and pure agreement; if this were the case, there would be no resonance at all. If I were to hear nothing but the same thing over and over again (or the same thing expressed even more intensely), or if I were to seek nothing but further corroboration of what I already felt and believed, then this could not be described as a resonant relationship to the world. As I understand it, resonance means listening to or being perceptive to someone or something entirely different. This can admittedly be irritating, but it's a matter of being touched by a different voice, in one form or another. We are all aware of this. It's not a secret skill that has to be learned. As experts in early childhood development have already shown, this is something that even infants are able to do. This is the moment when infants pause and listen and understand that whatever they're doing is part of an interactive exchange that will influence what happens next. A young child will make a noise, for instance, and then listen to learn how its caretaker responds!

This gives rise to the second moment of resonance: self-efficacy. My actions create a sort of connection with this other person. This feeling of connection is an important moment, and the basic form of resonance, as I understand it, involves *listening and responding*. Something reaches me and calls out to me, and I suddenly realize that a connection has been formed and that I'm now able to react to what has been received. You are perhaps familiar with this from certain situations that take place at the university or in church, or many of you are familiar with it from your schooldays or from working with children, or if you've ever had a chance to speak to a full lecture hall. In the latter situation, it can often feel as though you're speaking to a brick wall. You look out and see a bunch of apathetic and impassive faces or tired glances, or members of your audience are slumped over their phones or half asleep. Or, even worse, it's clear that the audience hates you because you've said the wrong thing or used gender-inclusive language or not – these days, one can get a good drubbing either way. However, you can also detect the precise moment when the conditions change for the better, when a new form of relationship emerges: Then you suddenly and literally see how resonance is created, when a certain idea is expressed that changes how people are sitting, focuses their gaze, causes eyes to light up, and sets something in motion. When efforts are made to measure what happens in moments like these – the Max Planck Institute for Empirical Aesthetics in Frankfurt does this very thing – the results are clear to see: When I suddenly stop and listen, when I allow myself to be touched by something, even my breathing will change, my heartbeat will change, the sensitivity of my skin will change, and the amount of hormones released into my body will change as well. We react to being called, we do something with it, and exactly then we begin to feel alive. In short, this is the moment of feeling alive. Bruno Latour, Corine Pelluchon, Andreas Weber, and many others have made this same observation. This moment of vivacity, of feeling alive, is precisely the moment at which I'm not only called or invoked or addressed but also when I suddenly realize that I can get something started with the voice that has reached me, with the music that I've encountered. Sometimes, however, we fail to achieve this experience. When this happens, we could even be listening to the most beautiful piece of music and think: This may be my favorite song, but (this time, at least) it isn't really touching me or moving me at all. Because, at the moment in question, I happen to lack this ability to respond, the ability to stop and listen, I'm unable to encounter something, open myself up to it, and do something with it.

However, in the event that you do happen to react, in a self-efficacious way, to being touched, this experience will instigate the third moment of resonance: the moment of transformation. Whenever resonance does take place – whenever I really stop and connect with what has touched me – I enter into a different state of mind and consider different ideas. I begin to see the world differently, or think differently. Now, it's also the case that when I feel deeply depressed or burned out, then I'm no longer capable of experiencing resonance. In fact, modern medicine has shown that depression clearly reduces our ability to be touched and affected; it also reduces our motivation and, with that, our expectation of achieving self-efficacy. Resonance is not about a sort of cognitively ascertainable meaning that somehow transcends the effects of burnout. In a sense, burnout is the opposite of resonance. Burnout is the state in which I'm no longer capable of experiencing resonance, in which I'm unable to be reached by anything and unable to affect anyone or anything myself. In this condition, I'm incapable of being invoked and I lack self-efficacy; I feel inwardly numb and even find it difficult to move. If, in contrast, I open myself to the experience of resonance and allow myself to be called or touched, then I also undergo an experience of transformation: I am no longer the same person, but rather someone who has been transformed in a moment of experience. This, to repeat, is the moment of feeling alive.

What's decisive in all this, however, is that the moment can't be forced. I can buy expensive tickets to the best concert and think: "Today it's going to happen!" When I went to my first Pink Floyd concert, for instance, I thought: "Today I'm going to experience enlightenment." But unfortunately that was not the case. I don't know why, exactly, but I found it boring. And I say this even though it sounds almost blasphemous to me; Pink Floyd remains my favorite band, and these were the heroes of my youth. When something like this happens, by the way, we often exaggerate and try to convince ourselves that the event in question was *insanely awesome* or *unbelievably good!* (But this is mostly because the ticket was so expensive.) In fact, I believe that the more people gush with ostentatious enthusiasm, the less resonance was actually experienced. It can't be forced – not with the most expensive tickets, not with a Northern Lights Promise, and not with the best setting. Candlelight dinners or Christmas are also rituals of this sort – that is, they are rituals with which we hope to control or dictate resonant moments. The expectation for this is perhaps greatest on Christmas Eve. Up until five o'clock, we're mostly in the mode of managing everyday exasperation, and then we suddenly (and punctually) want to enter into a state of resonance with our family, with the Holy Family, and with the message of the Gospels, but – to be honest – anyone who's been in this situation knows how things usually turn out: The potential for alienation and conflict is never greater than at this very point in time. This is because resonance cannot be produced, and certainly not by pushing a button. Most candlelight dinners fail to produce this effect as well; in reality, they somehow tend to lead to bickering instead of resonance. The fourth aspect of a resonant relationship is, therefore, its uncontrollability: Such a relationship cannot be created, bought, or forced.

When the opposite happens, however – when resonance really does occur – then, as I've already mentioned, a transformation will take place. Yet what's exciting about this is that no one can predict what will come out of it; no one can predict, in other words, what sort of transformation this will be. Let's take this evening as an example. Later, when we have a panel discussion, it's possible that I might say what I always say in response to a certain argument, because I've already done so a hundred times. And my fellow panelists might perhaps also say what they've already said over and over again, and then we'll all live with that outcome and the discussion will end without a resonant moment. It might also happen, however, that we manage to reach one another and then listen up and say: "I've never thought about it that way! That's an interesting idea!" Then something new will emerge; that said, it's important to stress again that it's impossible to predict, first, whether this will happen; second, when this will happen (if it does); and, third, what will come of it. Part of the uncontrollability of resonance is thus its open-endedness. Resonance is the wrong tool for those concerned exclusively with optimization. In the case of optimization, I already know the desired outcome in advance; I already know what numbers or parameters ought to be improved. In this context, my colleague Hans Joas has written at length about the *creativity of action*, but my favorite metaphor for the fourth aspect of resonance is in fact Hannah Arendt's concept of natality, which I've already mentioned. In the case of natality, a new idea or practice suddenly emerges – an idea or practice that I've never thought about before, and neither have you. Resonance is therefore the central locus for creating something new. This novel thought or practice, however, is beyond our control and impossible to foresee.

What, then, do we need in this society? I would argue that our society needs to rediscover its ability to be invoked and to experience the open-ended self-efficacy associated with this ability. This, however, presupposes a change in attitude or disposition; it presupposes that we can succeed in stepping out of our aggressive mode and, for a moment, stop asking things such as: "What's in it for me? What do I get out of the deal? What do I still want to achieve? What can I control? What am I in charge of? What am I not in charge of?" Perhaps one could say that we need to be stripped bare; we need to be touchable, but that also implies vulnerability. This, of course, is highly risky in a society based on competition and bent on growth. The first requirement, in any case, is to attain this particular attitude, but the attitude alone does not guarantee that resonance will occur. For this, we also need the appropriate social and material spaces.

And what I would like to claim now is that religions often do, in fact, have these very spaces, or at least that one of their core purposes is to make such spaces available. These spaces possess elements that can remind us that there's another possible way of relating to the world, a way that is not growth-oriented or intent on controlling things. You can notice this simply when entering a church, a chapel, or a temple: Pay attention to the physically palpable difference between entering a supermarket or your office, for example, and entering a cathedral. Your physical posture is different, your inner disposition is different, even the direction or intentionality of your being-in-the-world is different. Presumably, this is due to the fact that we switch from a mode of *agency* – active behavior – to a mode of *patiency*: a mode of receptiveness and perception. When we're in church, we don't have to achieve, govern, acquire, or control anything. When we enter a church, there's nothing that we have to control or take into our possession. The aggressive mode has no target there. Typically, we go there without any particular expectations: We're prepared to be touched by whatever comes our way. Of course, this isn't always the case. If I've had traumatic experiences in church or if I were a militant enemy of religion, I wouldn't go inside with this attitude; in fact, perhaps I would even want to rip the crucifix off the wall, so there's always that possibility. And if I were an educated culture vulture with a long list of church-related sights and attractions that I simply have to see, then I would probably maintain an aggressive approach to the world – the church and its tourist attractions would just be more things to check off my to-do list or must-see list. People who enter without such intentions, however, find themselves in a still and quiet spatial context in which aggressive attitudes fade away for a moment, regardless of whether they themselves are believers or not. Of course, I'm not arguing that churches, mosques, or temples are the only places that can incite a change of attitude or disposition. When standing on the shore of an ocean, for instance, we might experience a similar opening of the heart and body in response to the vast undulating expanses lying before us.

Beyond the material spaces that it has to offer, religion seems significant to me because it also provides many different elements – on different levels of being – of an alternative relationship to the world. Consider the concept of time – think only of hymns like "My Times Are in Thy Hands," or the liturgical year. About such things, my father would always say: "It's totally boring, nothing happens, it's all been the same for the last two thousand years." My response to this now would be: "That's the whole point! No innovation, no acceleration, no growth!" This conception of time is entirely different from our notion of it as an economic resource that is necessarily scarce and has to be translated into value.

Even more importantly, the crucial point seems to be that almost all religious thought and the best religious interpretations, from the widest range of traditions, are based on the idea of perpetuating resonant relationships. This was not at first clear to me as a sociologist when I was writing my book about resonance. I only learned about this after the fact because so many theologians brought it to my attention. Take the example of perichoresis, the Trinity. This concept underscores the resonant relationship among the Father, the Son, and the Holy Spirit – and, beyond that, it also denotes the relationship between God and the faithful. In my book, however, I did consider whether the Catholic religion might contain certain elements or qualities of resonance that are lacking in Protestantism, and I'm tempted to say: *Yes it does!* In Catholicism, ideas of resonance are more closely associated with material practices and bodily experiences than they are in Protestant churches. As a Protestant child, for instance, I was always slightly envious of my Catholic classmates, who would make the sign of the cross, dip their fingers in holy water, inhale incense, genuflect, light candles, or even pray to the saints. For me, this has never been about the cognitive content or "truth content" of such activities; they've simply always struck me as an embodied way of relating to the world. The idea behind all of these gestures and rites has always been about forming some sort of connection – a resonant connection with this world and with the world beyond. The idea is that something touches me and releases in me a transformative effect, and this is a shared experience. Of course, Protestantism embraces such ideas and relationships as well – all religions do – but it has intellectualized them and thereby suppressed them to some extent.

Incidentally, the desire for resonance in society in general is extremely high, and this goes far beyond religious contexts. In my opinion – an opinion corroborated by a very good dissertation on the topic by Hana Doležalová – almost all phenomena that are referred to as "New Age" or "Esoterica" can be interpreted as a deeply rooted longing for resonance and thus also as a sign that people have faith in resonance itself. People search for resonance in stones and herbs, brooks and mountains and in the stars; they want to regain resonant experiences from such things. "Yes, there's somehow a relationship between me and this gemstone," one hears, or between me and Bach flowers, or between me and healing water. Or: I have to protect myself from the evil eye and from mysterious earth rays. The reason why astrology and horoscopes remain so widespread and popular is not that they're remotely plausible from a scientific point of view or even that they offer a good model for explaining things. Most people who consult them justify this activity by saying something like: "I don't really believe in any of this, but nevertheless . . ." Nevertheless what? I think that astrology and horoscopes are so attractive to many late-modern people because they provide a sense that there's a connection – a resonant relationship – between that which surrounds the world (the cosmos, or all-encompassing reality) and our inner selves, our fates, our characters.

Religion derives its power from just such a sense, from the feeling that there's a sort of promise of resonance from on high, and the promise is as follows: What lies at the heart of my existence is not the silent, cold, hostile, or indifferent universe, but rather a responsive relationship. For me, this is the core of religious thought in the monotheistic religions, but probably in many other traditions as well, and certainly in Hinduism and Buddhism. But let's stick with Christianity for the time being. For me, its basic idea, to repeat, is that our existence is not defined by the cold mechanism of an indifferent universe or by pure chance or even by an inimical adversary; instead, the heart of our existence consists of a reciprocal relationship: "I have called you by name, you are mine." If that's not a promise of resonance, I don't know what is! Something has called me and referred to me even before I existed. Or visualize this idea: "I have breathed into you the breath of life." There are countless images of this sort in the Bible, which I therefore interpret as a singular document of crying out and calling to be heard in order to find resonance in the silent starry void.

And the Bible, along with faith and the church, provides this one answer, this one promise: There is an entity that has called *you* and *heard* you and will answer, even if we don't understand this response and even if it isn't forthcoming in the here and now. Resonance in itself is uncontrollable and unpredictable, as I've already said, even in the case of resonant relationships between people in the same room, but the decisive point about this promise is that we are all involved in a resonant relationship on an *existential* level. A palpable and even physically visible axis of resonance can arise from this, for instance in the posture of prayer; here, it's even possible to feel, physically, the supplicant's intention. As a sociologist, I often asked myself: "When people pray, do they direct themselves inwardly or outwardly?" And my fascinating realization was: it's in both directions at the same time! Prayer gives rise to this very axis of resonance from the bottom of our being to the farthest distances. Through prayer, according to Karl Jaspers, people forge a relationship between the fundament of their existence and the all-encompassing Other. The essence of my existence – to paraphrase Martin Buber – is a resonant relationship.

This is not, however, merely a theological idea; it is also a lived religious practice. Let's consider, for instance, the rite of the Eucharist. This is a rite that activates three axes of resonance at the same time: one between people (a social axis of resonance), one between people and things (a material axis of resonance), and one to the all-encompassing Other (an existential or vertical axis of resonance). The Eucharist, in other words, gives rise to a *communio*, a relationship between people and a relationship to the all-embracing whole.

Here, however, a word of caution is in order. The fact that religious thought and religious practice can have such resonant potential by no means implies that lived and, above all, institutionalized religion can actually activate and take advantage of it. As we all know from the history of religion, the opposite is often the case. Historically speaking, hardly any other entity has been a more effective resonance killer than the Christian church. But this is also true of other sorts of religious institutions and authorities. To be honest, I fear that the possibility of inhibiting axes of resonance might be just as intrinsic to religion as the potential to open them up. The obvious reason for this is the inherent uncontrollability of resonance, which means that the other side of this relationship and the quality of this relationship might never be "attainable." After all, one can never be sure about this – as is also clear from family relationships, for instance. The problem is amplified, however, when it comes to institutions and authorities.

This often results in attempts to manufacture controllability, thereby ensuring one's own self-efficacy within the relationship. "God" is then defined, catechized, and dogmatized, with the consequence that religious authorities will presume to know what "God is saying" and what "God wants." With this move, however, the vertical axis of resonance is brought to an end. The basic form of the relationship is then no longer one of open-ended *listening and responding* to an uncontrollable Other, but rather one of knowledge and implementation. Bruno Latour was therefore right to point out that to ask someone to state *what* he or she believes in is to signify the end of religion (in the sense of a resonant relationship). To assert what religion says is to transform it into a monstrosity.

Religious institutions – and especially those that are dogmatically and theologically concerned with preserving their "pure teachings" – can therefore quickly become monsters that not only kill the vertical axis of resonance but also, in doing so, cause social relationships to fall silent: "Because God says so . . . you must do this and not do that." Thus, at least potentially, the social relationship is not designed as a resonant relationship, but rather as one of merciless commandments, domination, and submission in the name of God. This is the opposite of resonance, and what is perfidious about this is that considerable social power is derived from something that is no more than a postulated and dogmatized vertical relationship of resonance. This explains the never-ending chain of sexual-abuse scandals in the Catholic church and in other churches, and the religiously grounded deafness to resonance in society also explains why religious institutions in many places often find it so difficult to grant women an equal voice and to accept homosexual love. Efforts to make the vertical dimension available and controllable apparently cause these institutions to close their hearts and become inherently "uninvocable" on the interpersonal level. What we find instead of a listening heart is thus a heart that is cold, soliloquizing, and deaf.

The conviction that one is carrying out God's will or obeying and enforcing "holy laws" can, in an extreme way, cause a person to be ready, willing, and able to ignore the voices, eyes, and faces of others. On the one hand, this explains the religious fanaticism that is still (partly) responsible for many wars and acts of violence today and leads many secular people to conclude that religions are the root of all evil in the world. On the other hand, however, it also explains why it is that modernity's history of violence, which I've already mentioned, was essentially carried out in the name of churches and was often religiously motivated. Believers who are extremely deaf to resonance when dealing with others (women, people of different faiths, people who love differently) often understand their own behavior to be an expression of their effective and responsive relationship to a "divine call." This is perhaps the greatest danger of religion.

Over the past few years, much has been said and written about this dark side of religion and churches, which is hostile to resonance. It is now out in the open – thank God! – and it has caused many people in Germany, for instance, to leave institutionalized churches in record numbers, leaving services emptier and emptier each day. It's therefore unnecessary at this point to reiterate these sad details to you. It's important for me to stress, however, that such deafness to resonance is not a necessary consequence or inherent feature of religion, but rather just one potential outcome. We should not forget about its other side, which is characterized by the possibility of experiencing resonance in religious relationships, by the possibility of being invoked, and by the possibility of being open to transformation. If, and as long as, we understand religion as a resonant event and not as a guardian and defender of ultimate truths, this understanding will serve as an effective instrument for preventing it from becoming a monster.

My concern in all of this is not about the question of whether it's reasonable to have faith, whether there is evidence for the existence of God, whether the Bible explains the world or is even God's word or anything along those lines. As a sociologist, I'm not only unable to answer these questions – I don't even know how to pose them in a meaningful way. I am concerned, instead, with the question of what sort of *relationship to the world* arises from or within religious practice, and my final word on the topic is this: Religion has the power – it has a reservoir of ideas and a ritual arsenal full of just the right songs, gestures, spaces, traditions, and practices – to unlock a sense of what it means to be called, to be transformed, and to live in a state of resonance. Without this sense, as I have argued, it is impossible for a living democracy to function.

If society loses this sense, if it forgets that this type of relationship can exist, then it's ultimately done for. And therefore my answer to the question of whether today's society still needs religion can be nothing but a resounding *yes!* Many thanks for your attention!